FAMILY EXPLORATION PERSONAL VIEWPOINTS FROM MULTIPLE PERSPECTIVES

A Workbook for

FAMILY THERAPY
An Overview

Sixth Edition

Irene Goldenberg
UCLA Neuropsychiatric Institute

Herbert Goldenberg
California State University, Los Angeles

THOMSON

BROOKS/COLE

Australia • Canada • Mexico • Singapore • Spain • United Kingdom • United States

Printed in the United States of America
3 4 5 6 7 07 06 05

Printer: R.R. Donnelley
Cover art: Jose Ortega/SIS

0-534-55759-7

For more information about our products,
contact us at:
Thomson Learning Academic Resource Center
1-800-423-0563

For permission to use material from this text,
contact us by:
Phone: 1-800-730-2214
Fax: 1-800-731-2215
Web: http://www.thomsonrights.com

Asia
Thomson Learning
5 Shenton Way #01-01
UIC Building
Singapore 068808

Australia/New Zealand
Thomson Learning
102 Dodds Street
Southbank, Victoria 3006
Australia

Canada
Nelson
1120 Birchmount Road
Toronto, Ontario M1K 5G4
Canada

Europe/Middle East/South Africa
Thomson Learning
High Holborn House
50/51 Bedford Row
London WC1R 4LR
United Kingdom

Latin America
Thomson Learning
Seneca, 53
Colonia Polanco
11560 Mexico D.F.
Mexico

Spain/Portugal
Paraninfo
Calle/Magallanes, 25
28015 Madrid, Spain

NOTE TO INSTRUCTORS

This workbook represents our latest attempt to aid students in their understanding of family therapy theory and practices by applying the principles and concepts to their own lives. Our goal is to stimulate students to think about themselves in the context of the family in which they were raised and to consider how those earlier experiences affected their current relationships. It will not provide a comprehensive portrait of personality or cover all aspects of family life, nor is it intended to do so. It may, nevertheless, when carried out conscientiously, prove to be a profoundly moving and fruitful experience for students and instructors reading their stories.

We've compiled over 300 student-tested questions, plus some class exercises, divided according to chapter topics in our text (*Family Therapy: An Overview*, Sixth Edition) and further divided by topics within each chapter. In our experience, most instructors find it useful to select a specific set of questions, depending on their judgment of relevance to their teaching goals, rather than asking students to answer every question. While we've tried to reduce redundant questions, sometimes answers may be repetitious. Should this be the case, students should be encouraged to pick other questions that avoid redundant responses. In our opinion, students should be allowed to skip questions that, for personal reasons, they wish not to answer.

Since honest responses to the questions can be self-revealing, students should be encouraged to keep the material confidential while they fill out this workbook, treating it as one would a personal journal or diary, and not sharing answers with family members or fellow students as they go through the process. If material arises that proves painful or difficult, and beyond what would be appropriate for instructor-student dialogue, the student should be encouraged to seek professional help, preferably utilizing a family therapy mode.

Irene Goldenberg

Herbert Goldenberg

PREFACE

This workbook is intended to help teach you about the theories, viewpoints, and perspectives of family therapy by encouraging you to examine your own family experiences. We believe the theoretical material will come alive and the entire learning experience will be enhanced and become more meaningful as you begin to comprehend how these concepts apply to better understanding your own family. We've provided what we hope are a series of stimulating questions to start you thinking about family life. The more effort you make, the more you're apt to get out of the exercises. Your instructor will likely select those questions he or she deems most important in maximizing your learning experience.

All families tell stories about themselves. We Millers love to argue, we Salingers adore children, we Changs have great memories, we Avilas are mathematically inclined. Typically such stories are passed along over generations and are adopted without challenge by new generations. You undoubtedly have your own set of stories heard from parents, grandparents, and other relatives.

Sometimes such stories are passed down as problems that require attention. The Peterson men are mean and self-centered. The Washington women always get involved with the wrong men. The Hardys have always been hard drinkers. The Smiths cannot take pain.

We would like you to use this workbook to investigate the stories your family has agreed to tell about itself, and especially how these stories affected the adult you became. Through a series of exercises, we hope you will scrutinize the myths and legends, truths and half-truths, realistic self-appraisals and self-deceptions, strengths and resiliency in your family, all in the service of aiding you in understanding many of the beliefs with which you grew up and which influenced your personal development. Should you require extra space beyond what we have provided in answering a question, simply insert additional sheets to complete your response.

If, as you proceed through these exercises, you find that you require further assistance or clarification, refer to *Family Therapy: An Overview,* Sixth Edition, by Irene Goldenberg and Herbert Goldenberg (2004). (The exercises in the workbook are organized according to the chapters in the text.) You can also refer to the original sources, listed in the Reference section of the text, for more detailed reading.

To gain the most from this workbook, you must be honest about yourself and your family. At times some of you may feel the questions are too personal, too exposing, too upsetting; those questions can be skipped. Ideally, however, this will rarely if ever be the case, and the workbook experience will act as a catalyst in your personal growth process. It may also serve as a vehicle for finding your strengths and weaknesses, comfort zones and blind spots, as a potential family therapist. Don't hesitate to share self-observations and insights, when appropriate, with professors, supervisors, therapists, parents, or significant others. (You also have the option, of course, of keeping the material confidential.) Should you develop "stuck places" or become troubled by patterns you discover about yourself, seek help from someone who thinks in systems terms, understands behavior emerging out of a family context, and who therefore speaks your language.

By learning more about yourself, especially by adopting a family perspective, we believe you can help others, future clients, see themselves within the context of their family lives.

Irene Goldenberg

Herbert Goldenberg

CONTENTS

CHAPTER 1

Adopting a Family Relationship Framework

Family Structure

1. Entrance into a family occurs by birth, adoption, or through marriage. Compare the characteristics of family membership (loyalty, support from others, closeness) of two people in your family, each of whom joined the family by different routes. How are they different and how are they alike?

2. Families today may be created by artificial or biotechnological means. If you or your partner were unable to get pregnant, which of the following extraordinary means would you be willing to employ?

Sperm bank
Artificial insemination
Donor eggs
None of these

Explain the basis for your choices.

3. In what type of family structure did you grow up—intact, one led by a single parent, stepfamily? Has divorce of a family member or members played a role in your life?

4. What are the expectations you have about the family structure you will be part of in five years? Twenty years? Forty years? Try to frame your answer around a discussion of your attitudes toward marriage, children, divorce, extended families.

Gender and Cultural Considerations

5. Family systems are embedded in a community and in society at large. Which of the following social or cultural factors do you believe were especially significant in your family of origin? Choose one or more and elaborate.

Race
Ethnicity
Social class
Sexual orientation
Religious orientation

6. Nowadays, cross-cultural and cross-racial adoptions are becoming more common. How would these phenomena have been viewed by the members of your family in the past, and what would have been seen as its advantages or disadvantages?

7. Americans tend to describe themselves as belonging to the middle class, and presumably are uncomfortable identifying others as being outside of that classification. However, people are likely to be more aware of class differences in dealing with one another than they readily admit. Describe an incident where you or a member of your family became aware of class differences in an exchange with another family.

Family Interactive Patterns

8. Shared family rituals help insure family identity and continuity. List some of the rituals you recall in growing up. Comment on the place and influence of those experiences in your later life.

Family Narratives and Assumptions

9. Most families have an outlook that perceives the world in general as a positive and predictable place or as a dangerous and menacing one. This perspective affects all family members. What was the general world view of your family when you were growing up? Did it change over time? How were you affected?

10. Was there a story or expectation in your family that encouraged or discouraged you from achieving (college is a must for girls in our family; business is the way to go for the men in our family; nobody ever makes good in our family)? Elaborate on its impact on your self-concept today.

Family Roles

11. Draw a picture of your family. Be sure to include all members. When you have finished, note what you see about your view of relationships, alliances, and coalitions in the family.

12. List in order of importance the roles that you currently play (son or daughter, friend, student, lover, neighbor, etc.).

1. _____   4. _____

2. _____   5. _____

3. _____   6. _____

Which of these roles are integral to your sense of self (ones you believe you cannot do without)?

Of all the roles listed above, which *one* would you insist on holding on to most strongly?

Of all the roles you have listed as currently playing, which would you find it easiest to give up?

Resiliency

13. All families face challenges: an unexpected death, the possibilities of divorce, job loss, retirement. What resiliency factors were available in a challenging situation in your family? How did the family reorganize itself, solve problems, and cope with threat?

14. Family resiliency can be a function of intact support systems: networks of friends, extended family, religious groups, community resources. Can you identify the support systems that helped your family in a crisis?

15. What experiences did you have as a child, in your family or school or community that contributed to your resiliency as an adult? Consider family organization, belief systems, and typical communication patterns in your answer.

16. What role did spirituality play in your family life when you were growing up? Comment on its impact on your current views about religion and spirituality.

17. Ambiguous loss of a family member, as demonstrated by the response of some relatives of victims of the September 11 terrorist attack on the World Trade Center, is a common reaction to a painful but unforeseen event. Have you or a family member been through such an experience? Describe.

Cybernetics

18. Provide an explanation of some behavior of yours that has been criticized by a significant family member—first in the language of linear causality and then in that of circular causality.

19. Consider a problem that exists or has existed in your family (say, an adult's drinking problem, or chronic unemployment of a parent, or a child who is a slow learner or one who refuses to go to school). Describe the problem as it is understood by your family.

Now rethink the problem as a possible product of a flawed relationship between two or three members. Describe.

The Identified Patient

20. At different stages of a family's life cycle, different members may be labeled the "identified patient" or the symptomatic person. Did this occur in your family? Who was so designated? Did you ever receive that designation? How did it affect your everyday behavior and your picture of yourself?

21. Is there currently an identified patient in your family, perhaps labeled "sick" or "bad"? Does this person drain off tension for the family, or distract from other underlying problems? How have you reacted?

How did this designation get established? How could it be changed?

What would happen to the interaction of the remaining family members if this person left?

22. Consider rewriting a particularly difficult family story. Do you experience differences in affect as you re-read the new narrative? Discuss.

CHAPTER 2

Family Development:
Continuity and Change

Your Family of Origin

23. How are relationships maintained across generations in your family? Do grandparents maintain a special place in your family with their grand-children? What is the significance of those relationships?

24. Discuss in systems terms the statement that grandparents and grand-children are friends because they have a common enemy.

25. In a marriage, each spouse usually acquires a set of roles and adheres to a set of rules, often unstated, for marital interaction. In your parents' marriage, do you believe these patterns enabled each individual to maintain a separate sense of self? Elaborate.

26. How does your expected role (as a husband, wife, or with a partner) differ from that of your same-sex parent? In what way were your socializing experiences related to this issue different or the same when you were growing up?

27. Comparing yourself with your same-sex parent at your age, what noteworthy differences in expectations exist (e.g., regarding family responsibilities, marriage, career moves, child rearing)?

Social Factors and the Life Cycle

28. What privileges or restrictions in your lifestyle were affected by your socioeconomic status growing up?

29. How much has ethnic identification given way to assimilation in your family? Elaborate on any benefits or losses to you and your family as a result of any changes.

30. In different cultures, children are expected to "leave the nest" at different ages. What was the expectation in your family?

31. How many generations has your family been in this country? How has this made an impact on your life?

32. Were you raised in a one- or two-paycheck family home? How did breadwinner status affect the power balance in the family?

33. What were the critical transition points for your family of origin (e.g., marriage, birth of first child, last child leaves home)? Were there one or more points of particular crisis involving the resolution of any of these tasks?

34. Describe the vertical and horizontal stresses around a crisis time in your family (death, illness, financial setback, moving to a new location).

35. How did the cultural background that each of your parents brought to their marriage blend or conflict with one another? What were the major consequences for the children?

Developmental Stages

36. In many families, adolescents are the focus of much attention, as if they and not the family system are the basis of family conflict. What was going on with your family members at the time of your adolescence that contributed to family harmony or disharmony?

37. Describe the stage of life your parents were in when you reached adolescence. How did this affect your adolescence?

38. Will you or have you left your family's home to live alone or with others? If so, how did your mother and father react to this stage in family development? Were their responses different from each other? How?

39. At what age do you think it is appropriate to get married? How have your background and family experiences shaped your attitudes toward marriage and its appropriate time in your life?

40. Do you know of a marriage where a new spouse had difficulty gaining entrance into the family circle of their marital partner? What personal and family problems derive from such circumstances?

41. How often should a newlywed couple visit or talk by telephone with their parents? How has your background shaped your thinking?

42. Have you personally witnessed the arrival of a child disturb the family equilibrium of a previously well established but childless couple? How? How did they cope with the imbalance? In what ways did husband and wife react differently? Did grandparents reenter the family system?

43. Have you experienced the death of a grandparent? Was it the first death where you were involved? How did the family handle it? What reactions of yours do you recall?

44. Overall, how has your family dealt with life cycle transitions? Did they deal with job changes, children leaving home, marriages, illness or death of family members with the same equanimity? Can you remember a transition that was problematic for the family? Was the family "stuck" for a period of time? How, and how well, did they move beyond the impasse? Are there residual consequences today?

45. Consider the issue of stress in your family. Did the stress first appear in your parents or grandparents? Were family patterns (drinking), attitudes (all the men in this family are weak) or secrets (grandma and grandpa never actually got married) passed on to you? What has been their influence on your outlook and expectations?

Alternative Families

46. Did you ever live in a single-parent-led family? If so, what were the significant consequences for the family (economic hardship, grief, loss of a support system, etc.)? Were there any family resilient factors that emerged?

47. From your own experiences, or just from speculation, what do you think would be the major family problems in a joint custody arrangement?

48. Have you known anyone raised by a gay or lesbian couple? Can you describe the family relationships during early childhood and during adolescence? Did you observe any special problems in this alternative family structure?

49. Was there someone gay or lesbian in your nuclear and extended family when you were growing up? Was his or her sexual preference out in the open or was it kept secret? How did it affect your family?

50. How has your own ethnic background, immigrant status, or financial circumstances affected your ability to leave home?

CHAPTER 3

Gender, Culture, and Ethnicity
Factors in Family Functioning

Gender Issues

51. Which of your parents played a more nurturing role in raising their children? Did this activity have high or low status in the family?

52. You often hear the phrase "It's a guy's thing." Discuss a recent incident you have experienced where gender might have provided an explanation of the behavior.

53. Discuss an episode of gender discrimination in your past. How did it affect you?

54. Did you grow up with same-sex or opposite-sex siblings or both? Where were you in the birth order? How did these experiences affect your attitudes regarding gender issues?

55. How was power distributed in your family? Who was in charge of what? What role did gender play in that assignment?

56. Who made the bigger adjustment in your parent's marriage? How was gender an issue?

57. List in two columns the values that had the highest and lowest valences in your family of origin. Include the following (and any others you wish to add) in your list.

Autonomy
Nurturance
Control
Independence
Relationships
Dependency
Caretaking

HIGH VALENCE	LOW VALENCE
_____	_____
_____	_____
_____	_____
_____	_____
_____	_____

58. Did your family approve of behaviors commonly associated with males or females equally, or was one emphasized over the other? How flexible were they about deviations from these behaviors? Explain.

59. Name and describe some ways in which a gender-based rule or sexist attitude or stereotypic sex role assignment affected the kind of adult you became.

60. Did your mother work outside the home? How did that affect the distribution of power in the family?

61. If you were a therapist, with what gender issues would a client family likely be concerned about you? Would such gender concerns be greater or less than concerns regarding your ethnicity, age, race, or experience?

Gender Role Training

62. What kinds of toys were you given as a child (e.g., dolls, trucks)? Did you play with them under a gender schema of what was considered masculine or feminine? To what extent did such play enhance or inhibit your development from a gender perspective? What kinds of toys will you give your children? Why?

63. Do you have a sustaining network of friends or family based on gender? Elaborate on their role in your life. Did either of your parents have such a network group?

64. What strengths, if any, have you acquired by bypassing traditional gender roles? Any special enjoyments from breaking the rules? Any significant mishaps?

65. How were your parents' child-rearing methods affected by their ethnicity or social class status?

66. What has been the impact of your family's socioeconomic or ethnic background on the development of your current attitudes regarding money, political affiliation, or sense of acceptance in mainstream American society? Choose one to discuss.

67. Did you grow up with people culturally and ethnically like yourself? If so, how did that contribute to your stability and sense of belonging? If you grew up in an environment where you felt different, how did that affect your sense of yourself and your acceptance by others?

68. Looking around at your community, with how many ethnic groups would you need to familiarize yourself in order to consider yourself a culturally sensitive therapist? Describe one or more of these groups with whom you have had the least experience.

69. Which social class best describes the one in which you grew up? Circle one.

Working class   Lower middle class   Middle class
Upper middle class   Upper class

How does this background affect your attitudes regarding class differences? Are there areas in your thinking that might affect your ability to work therapeutically with members of classes different from your own?

70. When, and under what circumstances did your family immigrate to this country? How did this event affect your current attitudes regarding immigration of others?

71. Which of the following were the most powerful influences in your family's functioning: ethnicity, race, social class, religion, stage of acculturation? Explain.

72. Crossing social class lines can be stressful. Can you describe any particularly noteworthy experience when you engaged in such activity (e.g., going to a country club, visiting someone in an impoverished neighborhood) and what its impact was on you?

CHAPTER 4

The Family as a Psychosocial System

Family Rules

73. All families have certain unspoken rules, such as: no discussion of sex; deny mother's drinking; never raise your voice; if you can't say anything nice, don't say anything at all. What were some of the rules in your family of origin?

74. How was money handled in your family when you were growing up? Who had the right to decide what about how it was spent? In what way is your handling of money different and in what way the same as what you experienced in your family of origin?

75. A "marital quid pro quo" is present in all couple relationships. Can you recount some of the rules your parents established? What about the rules in your current relationships?

76. According to Jackson, family members interact in repetitive behavioral sequences (the redundancy principle). Can you recall some significant, if not necessarily overtly stated, recurring patterns in your family of origin?

77. Scapegoats within a family go under many guises. Do you recognize any of these in your family?

____ idiot	____ mascot	____ wise guy
____ fool	____ clown	____ saint
____ malingerer	____ black sheep	____ villain
____ imposter	____ sad sack	____ erratic genius

Describe the behavior of one of the persons so labeled. What were the consequences for that individual later in life?

Maintaining Family Homeostasis

78. Crises occur in all families. Some are resolved relatively quickly, others linger. Describe two such situations in your family—one in which homeostasis was restored quickly, another in which resolution was more difficult.

79. Has separation of one family member from the others in your family provoked a family crisis? This can occur due to illness, death, vacation, business, war, etc. What happened? How was the homeostasis restored?

Family Feedback Mechanisms

80. How do you signal for attention with someone you care about? Verbally? Nonverbally? Is this tactic different or the same one you used as a child?

81. What kind of positive and negative feedback do you currently get from friends or family members? Be specific.

82. Trace the feedback loops that occurred after a misunderstanding between two members of your family. Was the subsequent exchange of information used to attenuate or escalate the problem?

83. According to the text, family stability is actually rooted in change. Was there a time when your family, called upon to cope with change, found it difficult to do so, creating instability and introducing a new set of problems?

Subsystems and Boundaries

84. Were you aware of important subsystems that existed in your family when you were growing up? Describe them. Were they organized primarily by generation, gender, alliance against another family member or faction, or by a similar dimension?

85. How permeable was the parental boundary when you were growing up? What effect did the relative openness or closeness of your family boundaries have on your development?

Open and Closed Systems

86. How would you assess the degree of openness of your family of origin? Were the boundaries open to neighbors? Distant relatives? Were your friends welcome or kept at a distance?

87. Sometimes a family will attempt to close a system when they perceive danger in the environment. What might the negative consequences of such action be? Draw from your own experiences.

Families and Larger Systems

88. What macrosystems were significant in the life of your family (church, social agencies, health care programs, etc.). Discuss.

89. When larger systems (e.g., the school) defined the problem of a family member differently than your family did, how did the family attempt to resolve the contradictions? How successful were they in doing so?

90. Try to depict your family graphically by creating an ecomap. Include the systems with which your family had contact (schools, medical services, churches, community centers, etc.).

CHAPTER 5

Origins and Growth of Family Therapy

Individual vs. Family Therapy: The Confidentiality Issue

91. Safeguarding the personal privacy of the therapist-client relationship has been a cornerstone of individual psychotherapy. Family therapy, in contrast, is sometimes observed or videotaped for later viewing by trainees and supervisors or by professional groups. This brings up the issue of confidentiality. What are your feelings about participating with your family under the conditions of family therapy?

92. How would you feel about sharing your "secrets" with your family members and a therapist? Any family taboo topics? How would you expect your parents to respond to questions about these topics?

93. Think of problematic behavior in a family member, such as periodic despondency or bursts of anger, and "explain" it at:

a. the individual level

b. the family level

c. the societal level

Family Dysfunction

94. Were any of the following patterns recognizable in your family of origin? Circle one and discuss its consequences for the other family members.

Marital Skew   Marital Schism   Emotional Divorce

95. "Emotional divorce" was an adaptive response to couple incompatibility that was probably more common before actual divorce became easier. What examples, if any, are you aware of in your family history? Would that same adaptation occur today? If not, why not?

96. Double-bind messages occur with varying frequencies in everyday life. Can you give an example of such a transaction from home, school, or work where you were double bound? What did you do? What was the accompanying affect? What would have happened had you tried to interrupt the sequence?

97. Analyze some problematic behavior of yours (e.g., nailbiting, smoking, overeating, swearing) from an intrapsychic and then a family relationship perspective. What has changed? Where is the locus of pathology?

98. Describe a family you know, saw on television, or read about in a book in which the members appear loving and understanding, but on closer observation are actually separate, distant, and unconnected. What happens to a child in such a family?

Individual vs. Group Therapy

99. What are your personal attitudes toward group or individual therapy? Which would be better for you? Why?

100. How would you feel about being observed through a one-way mirror as you interact with your family members? Would some members pose or try to be on their best behavior? Would others tend to dominate or control the session? What would your behavior be at first?

Self-Examination

101. Knowing yourself, if you were a family therapist, which would you be, a conductor or a reactor? Why?

102. Assume there is a symptomatic member of your family, who all agree is the identified patient. You all decide to attend a session if it would help that person. However, it soon becomes clear that the therapist is focusing on family interaction, not that individual's problems. How would you react? What would it take to persuade you to participate in further sessions?

103. How effective would family therapy be with your family of origin? Why?

104. Recount a cherished "truth" about your family that you believed as a child until a family member, friend, teacher, or book author later challenged you to consider whether it was an illusion.

105. A feeling that a therapist has the answer to a specific problem can be comforting and reassuring. Can you think of advantages that occur when the therapist takes a collaborative position, believing the family members themselves can find the answers they seek?

106. Has a new person entering your family (a minister, a daughter-in-law, a foster child, a visiting relative) helped its members re-evaluate their belief system?

107. Reflecting teams sometimes sit in the consultation room while family therapy is taking place, and sometimes observe the therapy behind a one-way mirror. Which would seem right for your family? Explain your choice.

108. In your opinion, which is preferable in helping families change: changing their structure or their language and belief system? Defend your position.

109. What spiritual or religious sources were or are present in your life to help determine your values, attitudes, and beliefs?

CHAPTER 6

Psychodynamic Models

Freud, Adler, Sullivan

110. Should family therapists emphasize the past or present, in your opinion? Explain your position.

111. Adler's theory stressed the importance of social elements in personality formation, challenging Freud's biologically-based drive theory. Which would your family have considered a better choice, theoretically speaking, in seeking help with family problems? Why?

112. Harry Stack Sullivan emphasized the "relatively enduring patterns of recurrent interpersonal situations" in personal and social development. Discuss such a pattern from your family of origin.

The Psychodynamic Outlook

113. Did scapegoating occur to one or more of your family members while you were growing up? What were the consequences of such a role designation? Are there current residuals in that person's relationships to the rest of the family?

114. Did any sudden role changes occur for any family member as you were growing up? What circumstances (e.g., death or disability of a major wage earner; widowed grandmother moved in) led to the changes? Describe how the various members of your family reacted.

115. If you presently are in a relationship that has developed problems, would it be better or worse if your spouse or significant other attended the psychodynamically-oriented sessions with you? Explain.

116. How would your family feel about coming to see a therapist whose theory was that failures in adult behavior were the result of poor experiences with inadequate or unavailable parents? Would the children and adults in the family react differently to this view?

117. Consider a current problem you may be experiencing and offer an explanation as to its origin from monadic, dyadic and triadic viewpoints.

118. Do you know of any special conditions surrounding your birth that would have encouraged or discouraged a particularly strong and enduring attachment to your mother? If so, what were the later consequences for you?

119. Consider the statement that an individual's capacity to function successfully as a spouse depends largely on that person's childhood relationships with his or her parents. Applied to yourself, what expectations might you have about your own marriage or other long-term relationship?

120. What "introjects" left over from early childhood are you aware of in yourself today? What impact do such imprints have on your current dealings with adults and children?

121. Observe two mothers with their infants. What differences do you notice about their attachments? What part does each play in maintaining the attachment? If the infant is securely attached, what effect might that have on his or her future adult relationships?

122. Consider a working mother who places her child in a day care arrangement. What would object relations theorists consider to be the potential problems? What is your view regarding this practice?

123. Does Fairbairn's concept of *splitting* (the child's internalized image of mother as a good object and as a bad object) shed light on anyone you know who has trouble in forming and sustaining satisfying relationships as an adult?

124. How would you and the members of your family feel about family-of-origin sessions such as those conducted by Framo? What kind of corrective experience might occur?

125. Describe some early family influences on the growth of your sense of Self? Be specific, listing ages and events.

126. Is there someone in your family or in the popular media whom you view as having a narcissistic personality disorder? Describe how this person views other people as extensions of his or her Self, existing primarily to serve him or her. Pay particular attention to this person's reaction to someone who is unresponsive.

CHAPTER 7

Experiential Models

The Symbolic-Experiential View (Whitaker)

127. Whitaker has been described in the text as iconoclastic—and sometimes outrageous—in dealing with families. He was unpredictable, and used humor, his own fantasies, and unconscious processes—even falling asleep—to contact and challenge his clients. How would your family respond to such an approach?

128. Have you ever experienced a time in your life when "acting crazy" was a liberating experience? Describe.

129. Which one of the following two approaches would your family of origin have felt best met its needs: a therapist who believed in dealing primarily with feelings or one who emphasized rational analysis?

130. As a follow up to the question above, would you now pick a therapist consistent with your family of origin patterns or one contrary to them?

131. How would you feel about having your grandparents (separately or together) in a family therapy session with you and your parents? What special problems would arise? What special advantages might there be?

132. The ability to talk "straight" (i.e., be authentic) is representative of therapists following the experiential model. Discuss your thoughts about the appropriateness of such an approach in reference to you and your family of origin.

133. Whitaker took the position that each person in therapy is to some degree a patient and therapist to one another. Discuss your reaction to this statement.

134. How comfortable would you be as a therapist disclosing personal aspects of yourself (your fantasies, impulses, images, or metaphors from your own life) to your clients?

135. Whitaker had a number of "rules" for "staying alive" as a human being and as a therapist, as described in the text. One was to "enjoy your mate more than your kids, and be childish with your mate." Was that true of your parents? Describe.

136. The use of co-therapy as an effective therapeutic technique has been debated. List some pros and cons and state your position.

Gestalt Viewpoint (Kempler)

137. How would your family react to a therapist's confrontational efforts to help them try to become more spontaneous and expressive of their feelings, both within the family and with outsiders?

138. Learning to communicate "I" messages is a basis exercise for Gestalt family therapy. For example, instead of an accusatory "You never pay attention to me!" an "I" message might be "I'm feeling ignored by you and it's upsetting me." Talk to a significant person in your life expressing "I" messages, and note how the transaction between you changes.

139. Which would be more comfortable for you and your family, a therapist who is self-revealing or one who is not? Why?

The Human Validation Viewpoint (Satir)

140. Satir stressed the mind-body relationship in her growth-enhancing, health-promoting therapeutic interventions. Discuss your own experiences with such body language connections (a pain in the neck, a stiff upper lip, etc.).

141. Satir classified family communication patterns in the following way:

Placater   Super-reasonable   Congruent   Blamer   Irrelevant

Describe a member of your family of origin or your current family using one of these categories, paying particular attention to that person's *characteristic* way of interacting.

142. Satir believed body posture reflects a great deal about an individual. In what way do you (or a member of your family) cover up true feelings when becoming distressed or feeling insecure? What physical pose do you assume under stress?

CLASS EXERCISE

Form a group of four persons in your classroom. Each should choose a new first name, then decide on a last name and assume a family role. Stay with your same sex role, but do not necessarily stay in your real life family (a son can be a father, etc.). Your communication should be as follows:

Pick a communication style and maintain it.

If you are a blamer, begin each sentence with statements such as "You are never" or "You are always." Find fault.

If you are a placater, take the blame for everything that goes wrong. Make sure no one gets hurt. Never say what you want.

The irrelevant one must not communicate in words properly. Be distracting.

The super-reasonable one must be stiff and proper. Stick to the facts, ignore feelings or greet them with statistics.

Have a five-minute discussion in front of the class. Stop. Relax. Report any messages you might be receiving from your body. What has happened in your new family? How did it make you feel? Share your impressions with one another and with the class.

Emotionally Focused Couple Therapy (Greenberg & Johnson)

143. You and a significant other are considering couple therapy to help reduce your quarreling. Would you prefer an object relations therapist who offers insight through interpretations or an emotionally focused couple therapist who acts as a facilitator to restructure negative interactive patterns? Explain your choice.

CHAPTER 8

Transgenerational Models

Family Systems Theory (Bowen)

144. Where do you fit, in relationship to your family, on Bowen's Differentiation of Self scale? Remember that people at the low end are emotionally fused to the family and thus are dominated by the feelings of those around them. At the other extreme of the scale, the high end, people are able to separate thinking from feeling and thus retain autonomy under stress.

Place yourself on the scale below and explain your answer.

1	25	50	75	100
Fusion				Differentiation of Self

145. What scores on Bowen's scale would you assign:

a. your mother?
b. your father?
c. your oldest sibling?
d. your youngest sibling?

Explain your reasons.

146. Triangulation is often noted in relationships among children. Can you remember a circumstance from your childhood when a third person was drawn into a relationship to decrease the intensity and stress between the dyad? What happened to the third person?

147. Bowenians contend that any of three possible symptomatic behavior patterns may appear as a result of intense fusion between the parents: physical or emotional dysfunction in a spouse; chronic, unresolved marital conflict; psychological impairment in a child. Did any of these patterns occur in your family?

148. Bowen believed that parents functioning at a low level of differentiation may transmit their immaturity to their most vulnerable, fusion-prone child. Did this or a similar family projection process occur in your family? Which child was most susceptible to such fusion? Explain.

149. Emotional cutoff in a family occurs when one member distances himself or herself from the others in order to break emotional ties. Distancing may take the form of a geographic move, unwillingness to attend family get-togethers, stopping talking to one or more relatives, etc. Has any of this occurred in your family? Was the problem resolved?

150. Bowen worked with the family in creating a family history (genogram) while Whitaker invited grandparents to join parents and children in a family session. Which would work better for your family? Why?

151. Make a genogram of your family, covering at least three generations. What have you learned about relationships within your family from the genogram?

152. Which of the children in your family, when you were growing up, was most fused to your parents? Can you speculate on why that particular child?

153. What is your sibling position in your family of origin? How does it match the sibling position of a significant person in your life (spouse, roommate, lover)? How do your corresponding positions growing up affect your current relationship?

154. Can you trace a specific dysfunction in your family (alcoholism, depression, anxiety attacks) back more than one generation?

155. Bowen advocated keeping down the emotional intensity in his work with families, so that the members might more easily think through what was causing their difficulties. Is there a member of your family who plays a similar role? Describe.

156. What resources can you find from the past history of your family that sustain or enrich your life today?

157. In your family ledger, what are some of the "unpaid debts" or restitutions that need to be made? If mother worked to put father through school, has she been repaid? Was there an imbalance in child-care responsibilities? Was that debt erased? If not, what are the residuals?

158. Family legacies dictate debts and entitlements. What legacies did you inherit? Were you expected to be an athlete, a musician, a scholar, a failure, beautiful, etc? How have you carried those legacies into your current relationships?

159. To function effectively, family members must be held accountable for their dealings with one another. How does your family balance entitlement and indebtedness?

CHAPTER 9

The Structural Model

Structural Family Theory

160. Structuralists contend that a change in the family organization must occur before a symptom in a family member can be relieved. Has such a situation occurred in your family? Who manifested what symptom and what family restructuring helped alleviate the problem?

161. Each family system is made up of a number of interdependent sub-systems. Were the key subgroupings in your family according to age, sex, outlook or common interest? Explain.

162. Has anyone in your family ever exhibited psychosomatic symptoms? How did the family deal with the problem? What homeostatic devices were activated whenever that person became ill or developed symptoms?

163. Is there any conflict between subsystems in your family that is particularly damaging or destructive to overall family functioning (e.g., older people dismiss what younger people have to say; females believe men are insensitive)?

164. Under stress, does your family become more enmeshed or more disengaged? Describe and explain the behavioral consequences.

165. Structuralists contend that all well-functioning families should be organized in a hierarchical manner, with the parents exercising more power than the children, the older children given more responsibilities than their younger siblings. Was this the case in your family of origin? What were the consequences of the power arrangements when you were growing up?

166. Some feminists take exception to Minuchin's insistence that a well functioning family requires hierarchies, arguing that this view runs the risk of maintaining sexual stereotypes. How was your family organized? Was there a rigid or flexible organization? Did it promote sexual stereotyping?

167. Do you consider the boundaries in your family of origin to have been clearly defined, rigid and inflexible, or diffuse? What were the consequences on family transaction patterns as a result of such boundaries?

168. Describe an incident of triangulation in your family. How was it resolved?

169. What coalitions can you remember in your family of origin? How constructive or destructive were their consequences?

170. Structuralists use family mapping to depict a family's structure at a cross-section of time. Using Minuchin's symbols described in the text, draw a map of your family at a particular critical time in its existence, paying special attention to the clarity of boundaries, to coalitions, and to ways of dealing with conflict.

171. Reframing the meaning of certain behavior can provide a fresh perspective and make that behavior more understandable and acceptable. Reframe the following:

a. Mother pokes into my private matters too much.

b. Father frightens the family when he drinks too much.

c. Sister is selfish and only thinks of herself.

d. Brother gets away with murder because he's the youngest child.

172. How does the reframing in the previous question change your feelings about the troublesome behavior?

CHAPTER 10

Strategic Models

The Communications Outlook

173. Describe the sorts of relationship definitions (symmetrical or complementary) you tend to get involved in with two of the following groups:

a. your male friends

b. your female friends

c. your parents

d. younger people

e. older people

174. Was the communication pattern between your parents primarily symmetrical or complementary? How did it enhance or constrict their relationship? Illustrate.

175. Discuss an important message you have received from your mother that was "encoded." Translate the message and describe your response.

176. You have an argument with a friend. Discuss how each of you is likely to punctuate the communication sequence.

177. A family member refuses to talk to you, but he or she is communicating something. What do you observe?

178. Your roommate says "It's hot in here." What are the content (report) and relationship (command) aspects behind the statement?

179. Describe a double-bind situation in which you have been caught. Remember that you must have a close relationship with the person, must respond, and are receiving messages at two levels. What did you do?

180. Describe an unsolved problem in your family. What makes the behavior persist?

Brief Family Therapy

181. At what point in your life could you and your family have benefited from brief (six-session) crisis intervention? (For example, you might consider divorce, death, drugs, alcohol abuse, school separation, or an auto accident as possible crisis times.) Describe the situation and explain why you believe such intervention might have been helpful.

182. A friend has a problem stopping smoking. How would you "prescribe the symptom"? What consequences would you anticipate?

183. Which would feel more comfortable to you as a family therapist: defining the family's problem before the session starts, or getting your cues from their unfolding discussion? Why?

184. As a therapist, how would you feel being observed behind a one-way mirror and being guided by an observing team?

The Strategic Viewpoint

185. Haley believes that symptoms are indirect strategies for controlling a relationship while at the same time denying that one is voluntarily doing so (e.g., mother becomes ill and can't be left alone when her adolescent daughter wants to go out for the evening). Can you cite an example from your own experiences?

186. Implicit in every relationship is a struggle for power, according to strategists. What power struggles are you currently experiencing?

187. Suppose a friend of yours drank too much or ate too much, and came to you for help in ridding himself of such excesses. Can you think of a therapeutic double-bind, a symptom prescription, or a paradoxical intervention to aid in reducing or eliminating the symptom?

188. Describe a current dyadic relationship you are in, and consider whether a third person is also somehow involved. Can you locate the triadic interaction?

189. In strategic therapy, the therapist is responsible for initiating change. How does that strike you as the client?

CHAPTER 11

The Milan Systemic Model

The Systemic Viewpoint

190. Bateson defined information as "a difference that makes a difference." What new information introduced into your family (perhaps through talking openly about a family secret) might have changed family members' behavior toward one another? Speculate on the changes.

191. Do you know of families whose unacknowledged "rules of the game" allow them, together, to control one another's behavior? Describe their efforts to perpetuate such "games." How effective is this maneuver in sustaining their family relationships?

192. You finally persuade your family to come for family therapy, hoping the therapist will expose the family "games" which only you seem to acknowledge. Instead, she offers positive connotations about behavior patterns you believe are destructive, and she warns the family about premature change. How would you react?

193. What would be the effect on you and your family of attending a therapy session while being observed from behind a one-way mirror by a team? How would you react to the intersession in which the therapist leaves the family alone while consulting with his colleagues?

194. Write a "paradoxical letter" to a member of your family who has refused to join the others in attending family therapy sessions.

195. Systemicists use interviewing techniques to interrupt and change family "rules of the game." Describe a dominant and long-lasting rule in your family of origin and speculate on what it would take to change it. Who would be most upset by the change?

196. How were rituals celebrated in your family? For example, was the person celebrating a birthday treated in a special and predictable way to mark the occasion? Were symbols (cards, gifts, ceremonies, family dinners) a part of the ritual?

197. What were the rituals surrounding the evening meal in your home when you were young? Did you eat together regularly? What topic could be discussed? What topics were off limits and avoided? Did people sit in special places on a regular basis? Who was served first?

198. Rituals often play a central role in family life, marking passages and changes. Prescribing rituals may help a family restructure how its members perceive events. In your family, describe a ritual (wedding, birthday party, graduation, funeral) that helped your family negotiate a change.

.

199. What circular questioning might be thought provoking for your family (e.g., "Who first noticed that?" or "Who enjoys fighting the most?")?

200. Choose one of Tomm's reflexive questions to address your family. How do you imagine they would respond?

CHAPTER 12

Behavioral/Cognitive Models

The Cognitive Viewpoint

201. Select a family problem you have discussed earlier in this journal and restate it in cognitive-behavioral terms.

202. Cognitive psychologists pay special attention to how individuals organize, store, and process information. Consider a problem you may have had for a long time, and put it into words at these three levels: Automatic thoughts, underlying assumptions, and schemas or basic core beliefs.

203. Dysfunctional behavior is said by Ellis to be a result of our flawed or illogical interpretation of the behavior of others. Use the concept of cognitive restructuring to deal with a problem you currently are having with someone. Create a new self-statement.

204. Is there a "negative schema" acquired in your childhood that has been reactivated recently? Describe.

205. Cognitive-behaviorists stress the importance of self-regulation and self-direction in altering behavior. What would be the pros and cons of this approach for you and your family?

206. Describe an incident where you heard one side of a story, then were startled later by hearing the other side. How did you resolve the disparity?

207. Take a recent speech of a politician and see if you can find:

a. arbitrary inferences

b. overgeneralizations

c. dichotomous thinking

d. biased explanations

208. Try to shape someone's behavior by giving that person positive reinforcement (a smile, a kiss, a gift, attention) whenever desired behavior occurs, while ignoring undesired behavior. Continue to do so for seven days. Describe your results and draw conclusions.

209. Behaviorists sometimes use the phrase "quid pro quo" (something for something) to describe how couples in successful marriages work out suitable arrangements for exchanging pleasures. Take a look at your parents (or an uncle and aunt) and describe the range and frequency of reciprocal positive reinforcements they exchange.

210. Create a "caring days" list with a significant other in your life. Be specific in your requests and ask the other person to be the same. Exchange the lists. After one week, note any changes in the relationship.

211. Were there any surprises in the "caring days" requests you received in the preceding exercise? How did such unexpected requests alter your perception of the relationship and/or change your subsequent behavior?

212. Would a contingency contract have been helpful in resolving any conflicts you may have had with your parents when you were an early adolescent? Describe the problem briefly and set up a contract.

213. Did your parents use informal methods of reinforcing desired behavior (e.g., promising a bicycle if your grades improved significantly)? How well did such methods work? Did they create any problems?

214. Where did your parents' marriage fall in relation to Gottman's couple schema: volatile, validating, conflict-avoiding? How well did it work?

Functional Family Therapy

215. Functional family therapists regard an individual's behavior as always serving the function of creating specific outcomes in that person's interpersonal relationships. Observe a friend or family member over several days, noting behavior patterns (without regard to whether you consider them desirable or undesirable), then speculate on the function of the behavior.

BEHAVIOR   FUNCTION

_____   _____

_____   _____

_____   _____

_____   _____

216. Consider a seemingly dysfunctional pattern between two members of your family, but one that nevertheless has persisted. What interpersonal payoffs might exist for the participants that help perpetuate the pattern?

Conjoint Sex Therapy

217. What was the dominant sexual theme transmitted to you by your parents (e.g., sex is a natural and enjoyable part of life; sex is to be endured; sex is not to be discussed)? What has been its impact on your current attitudes toward sex? What attitudes do you expect to transmit to your children?

218. Under what circumstances would you go to a counselor for sex therapy? Would you be expecting psychological or medical interventions

219. Has anyone in your experience been able to help you achieve "narrative repair" by changing your assumptions and schemas about the world as well as your ability to manage stress? How did they "coach" you to do this? What new narratives did you create?

CHAPTER 13

Postmodernism and the
Social Constructionist Therapies

Social Constructions

220. How would your mother describe you to a friend in your absence? Would your father agree? Would a friend concur?

221. Postmodernists consider constructions regarding reality to be based on language and communication. Has anyone in your family identified himself or herself, or been identified, as an alcoholic? How did that self-imposed label structure how others viewed and reacted to that person's problematic behavior?

222. Who in your family was most upset following the death of a family member? Who appeared to be least affected? Check with another family member about whether he or she agrees with your observations.

Discuss any differences in perception that arose from this exercise. Did you learn something?

223. Catch someone significant in your life doing something right. Comment on it. How did it change your relationship with that person?

224. Watch a TV sitcom and choose a character who is at an impasse in solving a particular problem. As a therapist, what might you suggest to help that person become "unstuck?" Does he or she seem to possess the knowledge or resources to get "unstuck?"

225. Different opening remarks by a therapist are likely to establish different sets and thus elicit different responses from a family. How would your family respond to each of the following?

a. Tell me what problems brought you to see me today?

b. How can we work together to help change your situation?

226. What do you consider to be the advantages and disadvantages of having a five or ten session limit to family sessions?

227. In your family, who would be the visitors, complainants or customers for therapy? Explain.

228. Can you identify a time when someone helped you re-story your life so that you saw the same events in a new and more positive light? What were the consequences? Did you feel empowered?

229. Consider someone in your life who always talks "problem talk." How could you help that person engage in "solution-talk?" Give an example and indicate anticipated effects of the change.

230. Answer this version of the "miracle question" for yourself:

Suppose that one night there is a miracle and while you were asleep the problem that you have been worrying about is solved. How would you know? What would be different? What would you notice the next morning that would tell you a miracle had occurred? What would your best friend notice?

231. Lynn Hoffman says that "problems are stories that people have agreed to tell about themselves." Write up one of your current problem areas from this perspective.

Now write an alternate story to the above. What has changed?

232. Rate a specific family problem on a ten-point scale, with 1 representing the least troublesome and 10 the most. Next, without revealing your rating, ask a family member to rate the severity of the same problem. Compare your scores and discuss the differences in viewpoint your scores reveal.

CLASS EXERCISE

Have a small group of students discuss a problem while the rest of the class, acting as a reflecting team, observes them. Then have the small group watch as the class discusses reactions to what they observed. Reverse the process once again. What did you learn?

CHAPTER 14

Narrative Therapy

233. Consider one of the "stories" told and retold in your family. How did its content shape your life?

234. How did the above story become established for you as the "truth?"

235. Was there a negative, self-defeating story told in your family as you were growing up? Describe.

236. Did your family of origin tell stories related to their ethnic, racial, or social class background? Discuss.

237. Discuss which of the following most shaped your current beliefs: historical, political, or cultural forces.

238. Was a "thin" description of you ever imposed by others (parents, clergy, teachers) in your life when you were young? Discuss.

239. What things must you keep in mind in honoring the stories and cultural background of a client family?

240. What is the role of a collaborative partner in family therapy? How is it different from the role played by a traditional family therapist?

241. Describe a primary self-narrative in your life (e.g., "my illness as a child made me introspective," "my grandmother's business success inspired me," "my mother's craziness made me wary of close relationships").

242. Discuss a dominant narrative of your culture (e.g., "a woman can't be too rich or too thin," "men wear the pants in the family," "such and such a group is inferior to us").

243. How has society controlled you with its definition of what it means to be a "real man" or "real woman?"

244. Who outside of your parents (extended family members, clergy, doctors, therapists) held the most power in determining what was true and proper in society?

245. Which one of the following political forces has most affected your life: racism, sexism, class bias, gay bashing)? Discuss.

246. Externalization often has the therapeutic effect of objectifying a problem and placing it outside the family in order for family members to begin to create alternative narratives. Consider a problem in your family, indicate how it might be externalized, and speculate on the consequences.

247. Describe a "problem saturated" story or self-defeating narrative that is told in your family. How does it reflect despair, frustration, or a sense of powerlessness?

248. Is there a subjugated story hiding in the above narrative? Retell the story from this new perspective.

249. Think of a problem you have had in your family where the attempted solutions always seemed to bring more trouble. Can you identify a "unique outcome," a time when you took some action and the problem did not get worse? What was the difference about that set of circumstances? What can you learn from the experience?

250. How would you feel if you had a problem and your therapist asked you about bringing in an "outside witness group?"

251. What would it feel like to receive a summary letter following each therapy session you attended?

252. If you had a family member reluctant to attend a family session, how would he or she respond to a "letter of invitation?"

253. Write a "redundancy letter" to a family member informing him or her that they no longer need to take the role they have been playing with you (e.g., an older sister playing mother).

254. Discuss how membership in a "league" might be useful in developing an alternative view of a problem in your family (e.g., anorexia, depression, alcoholism, chronic illness).

CHAPTER 15

Psychoeducational Family Therapy

Psychoeducation vs. Psychotherapy

255. Psychoeducational family therapy emphasizes interpersonal skills-building, a technique especially suited for dysfunctional families. Can you think of a family you know where such an approach would be the treatment of choice? State your reasons.

256. You visit your therapist and notice a manual on her desk from which she has been working with you and your family. What is your reaction? Explain why.

257. Following up the previous question, suppose you discover that your therapist has written the manual with a group of other professionals. Does that change your attitude?

258. One result of chronic mental illness may be seen in the streets and alleys of our cities. Where are the families of these people? How would you address the problem of mentally ill homeless men and women?

259. Have you known a family where a member has been diagnosed with a chronic mental illness such as schizophrenia? What did you observe about family functioning?

260. Is your family a high EE (Expressed Emotion) family or a low EE family? If high, is the emotional expressiveness characterized by critical language? Describe and discuss the effects on you growing up?

261. Is it possible your family might come for psychoeducational help but not for psychotherapy? Discuss.

Medical Family Therapy

262. Has there been a medical problem that affected the life of a member of your family? What kind of help of a psychological nature might have helped the family? the afflicted person? What kind of help did the family actually receive?

263. Medical family therapy is an interdisciplinary team approach. What would be the pros and cons in that way of working for you?

264. According to the text, "no biomedical event occurs without psycho-social consequences." Discuss this statement in reference to an experience in your family.

265. Do you know of a friend or family member who has AIDS? What has been the family's reaction? Did they offer support that the patient effectively utilized?

Short-term Educational Programs

266. How would you feel about taking a marriage preparation course with your significant other? What would you expect to learn?

267. Your church, mosque, or synagogue requires you to undergo one to three sessions of premarital counseling if you wish to be married there. A good idea or a bad one? Explain.

268. Do you know of couples in your family who could benefit from a brief course in relationship enhancement? Would they be willing to participate? What would be most beneficial in such a program?

269. You and your significant other arrive at a therapist's office for premarital counseling and are each handed a psychological inventory to fill out. What kind of feedback would you expect from the therapist?

270. Some ethnic groups exert considerable influence over the choice of marriage partners of its young people by matching individuals to one another or by forbidding marrying outside of the group. How does your own cultural background affect your thinking about this practice?

271. If you have lived in a stepfamily situation at any time, would a preparation course prior to forming the stepfamily have been helpful? How?

CLASS EXERCISE

Learning new patterns for resolving one's family problems may come from observing another family deal with an analogous problem. In Marriage Encounter weekends, couples have an opportunity to observe other married people attempt to solve their problems. Visit one of these programs and report back to the class on what you identify as the major change agents.

CHAPTER 16

Family Therapy Research

Research on Severe Mental Disorders

272. You are doing a research study on dysfunctional families and need a normal baseline for comparative purposes. How would you go about defining a "normal" family?

273. How would you rate your own family in terms of communication deviance when you were growing up? Would you say the rating changed over time?

274. Would you describe your role in your family of origin as more that of a *therapist* (actively intervening in family functioning) or a *researcher* (observing, classifying, and evaluating what was transpiring)? How did that earlier role influence your current interests?

Discovering Family Paradigms

275. Which of Reiss's family paradigms (environmentally-sensitive, interpersonal-distance-sensitive, or consensus-sensitive) comes closest to how your family of origin constructed reality? Illustrate how they dealt with a crisis, based on the type to which you assigned them.

276. If your family were to come for family therapy, would you want the therapist to diagnose them? If yes, should the therapist share the diagnosis with the family? If no, why not?

277. Observe the structure of the place where you work or attend school. Would you characterize the climate as rigid or flexible, autocratic or democratic, competitive or cooperative? How does this climate affect your functioning?

278. Observe a family planning something that they will do together (go to a movie, a restaurant, or vacation destination, etc.). How much information can you gather about the power structure, communication patterns, and type of family functioning? Discuss.

Family Therapy Research

279. What aspect of family therapy research would you like to continue to explore? Research methodology? Theory building? Classification and assessment? Process or outcome research? Explain your position.

CHAPTER 17

Becoming a Family Therapist:
Training and Supervision

Obtaining Clinical Training

280. Should a family therapist in training be required to undergo a therapeutic experience with his or her family? Take a position on this issue and defend your point of view.

281. Which should be taught first—individual therapy or family therapy? Why?

282. Is it important for an individual therapist also to be trained in family therapy? For a family therapist also to be trained in individual therapy? Explain your viewpoint.

283. What training would be particularly important for you in the areas of gender, ethnicity, or social class considerations? Explain.

284. Family therapy can be viewed as a profession, an orientation to human problems, or simply another therapeutic modality. Which outlook most closely reflects your position? Explain.

285. How would you feel, as a family therapist in training, about being videotaped conducting a session with a family? Compare your expected feelings about presenting the videotape to a supervisor versus presenting her with a verbal report of the session.

286. Having surveyed the various approaches to family therapy described in the accompanying text, which holds the greatest appeal for you? Why? Consider both intellectual content and style of treatment in your answer.

287. What personal qualities of yours are your greatest assets in becoming a family therapist? Do you have any special qualities that may hinder your effectiveness with families?

288. If you were receiving live supervision as you worked with a family, which of the following would be most comfortable for you? Why?

a. Telephone call from supervisor who offers suggestions
b. Bug-in-ear as you conduct a session
c. Supervisor enters the room
d. Calling you out during a session for consultation with a team that has been observing you and your client family.

289. Would you prefer to work alone with a family or with a co-therapist? Explain. If you had a co-therapist, what personal qualities would be important for that person to possess? Would the sex of your co-therapist matter? Why?

290. Some client families are more anxiety-provoking for some therapists than are others. What kinds of families would be most difficult for you to work with (e.g., aggressive, silent, secretive, demanding)?

291. What kinds of families would you feel most comfortable working with? Consider such factors as social class, communication style, religion, sexual orientation.

CHAPTER 18

Professional Issues and Ethical Practices

Licensing and Clinical Practice

292. In seeking professional help, what questions would you ask a potential provider regarding his or her training, professional experiences, and licensing?

293. How would you go about selecting a family therapist for yourself and your family? Would you seek out any specific discipline? What fee would you expect to pay? Should that fee be more than for an individual session?

294. Family therapy practitioners receive their training in a variety of disciplines (psychology, psychiatry, social work, counseling, the ministry). How would this professional background affect the choice of therapist for you and your family? What factors did you consider in making a choice?

Managed Care

295. Your family's health insurance is handled through a managed care arrangement. You select a therapist from their provider list, but are told that confidentiality cannot be guaranteed absolutely, since after several sessions the therapist must report details of the treatment to a case manager in order to receive authorization to continue. How would you respond? What are your options?

296. For what situations would you as a family therapist seek peer review?

297. What do you see as the pros and cons of managed care for you and your family?

298. Your therapist sends you an informed consent agreement prior to starting therapy. Some of the items, such as reporting child or elder abuse, seem unrelated to your problem. How do you proceed in completing the form?

299. Is sexual intercourse between a therapist and client ever justified? Explain your point of view.

300. What are your views regarding therapist record keeping? Would you feel comfortable as a client if the therapist took extensive notes during the session? Brief notes? No notes at all?

301. Suppose you as a therapist find out from a family that they were seen previously by a therapist who, according to their statements, abandoned them when they could no longer afford treatment. What are your professional responsibilities in this matter? What are your options? How would you proceed?

302. You tell a therapist you are seeing together with your family that you cannot afford his fee. He says not to worry, that he will bill your insurance company as though each member came to see him separately, and the total billing will more than pay for the sessions. Would you agree to this plan? If not, what would you do?

303. What strong religious, political, or philosophical attitudes or values do you hold that might affect your functioning as a family therapist?

304. A client asks you if what he is about to tell you will be kept in confidence. If not, he adds, he will not divulge the information. Can you guarantee confidentiality? If not, what would you say?

305. Are there some family secrets that should remain secrets? What are they? What family secrets must be exposed?

306. You receive a call from an adolescent girl in a family you are treating. She asks for a separate individual session this one time. What do you do? Why?

307. Looking back, has there ever been abuse present in your family? What were the circumstances? How was the matter handled? Was it reported to the authorities? Who participated in the final decision about what to do?

308. A friend of yours thinks he might have AIDS and wants to speak with a therapist but is fearful about the information being exposed. How would you counsel him to proceed? Include a discussion about whether he should use his health insurance policy in this case.

309. A close friend informs you that she had sexual intercourse with her former therapist, and asks you if you think she should tell her current therapist. What do you advise? Why?

310. You and your partner have come for couples therapy. At the end of the first session, the therapist hands you a statement about the duty to warn and about the limits of confidentiality. How would this act affect your decision about continuing therapy?

311. Your therapist tells you he is in his last year of supervision and thus cannot guarantee confidentiality since he must discuss the session with his supervisor. How would you respond? How would your fellow family members react?

CHAPTER 19

A Comparative View of Family Theories and Therapies

312. What have been the most important things you have learned about yourself and your family from these exercises?

313. Have you moved from an individual understanding of behavior to a systems view? If so, how have you changed your narrative about yourself?

314. Have you attempted any new solutions as a result of your changing outlook? If so, how successful were you in bringing about a desired outcome? Be specific.

315. Discuss periods of both optimal and disruptive functioning in your family as you were growing up, and explain their occurrence in systems terms.

316. Describe a time your family "got stuck" in a faulty solution to a problem. How was it explained then and how do you see it now?

317. Describe a dysfunctional marriage you have observed. Was there evidence of negativity, such as criticism, contempt, stonewalling or defensiveness? Describe.

318. Describe an optimizing couple. How is their functioning different from the couple in the previous question?

319. Discuss from the vantage point of your personal experiences whether insight or action has been more helpful in producing desired change.